LIFE CHOICES
and LIFE PATHS

EDWARD CRAVEN

ISBN   Softcover   978-1-951469-33-7

Printed in the United States of America.

To order additional copies of this book, contact:
BookWhip
1-855-339-3589
https://www.bookwhip.com

CONTENTS

ACKNOWLEDGEMENTS

A book is a collaborative team effort among many people. I thank the BookWhip team for their input, feedback, and suggestions that made this book better.

The topics in each chapter may surface reflections, thoughts, and feelings that the reader may wish to capture on paper. At the end of each chapter, there are pages with blank lines to write your reflections, thoughts, and feelings. This idea came from Ethel White, my Consultant – Publication and Marketing at BookWhip.

PREFACE

Think of this book as a journey of discovery to learn more about yourself and the principles, values, and priorities that you wish to guide your life. Individual freedom provides choices. Every choice has a consequence. The choices you make will determine the life paths you travel as well as the people, places, and things you will experience on your life journey.

The topics in each chapter may evoke reflections, thoughts, and feelings that you may wish to capture on paper. At the end of each chapter, there are pages with blank lines to write your reflections, thoughts, and feelings. I encourage you to use these pages to enhance your experience with this book.

I hope this book not only helps provide guidance and direction in your life but also is a tool in creating a life that you find worth living.

The idea for this book came from God. Each day that I worked on this book, I prayed for God's guidance and direction.

PREFACE

INTRODUCTION

This book presents two possible life paths – a path based on the Seven Deadly Sins and a path based on the Fruit of the Spirit.

The Seven Deadly Sins are laziness, gluttony, greed, envy, lust, anger, and pride.

The Fruit of the Spirit from Galatians 5:22-23 (New Century Version) are self-control, goodness, patience, joy, kindness, faithfulness, gentleness, peace, and love.

I hope this book blesses your life in some way.

I enjoyed writing this book.

I hope you enjoy reading this book.

CHAPTER 1

Ethel White, my Consultant – Publication & Marketing at BookWhip, has the following message in her email: "A dream does not become reality through magic; it takes sweat, determination, and hard work."

I have had to work on laziness in my life. If I was interested in something, I would give a better effort and vice versa. My mother helped in my development by asking the following question: Did you do the best of which you were capable?

Bob Knight was the head basketball coach at the University of Indiana and Texas Tech University. His definition of discipline is: "Discipline is doing what you need to do, doing it when it needs to be done, doing it to the best of your ability, and doing it that way all the time."

After years of working to improve in this area on all projects, I have developed a commitment to do my best. There may be people more talented in some areas than me and that is ok. I don't have to be perfect or number one in all areas, but it is important that I have done the best I can do. Today, I experience satisfaction when I have followed Bob Knight's definition of discipline and when I have completed the work to the best of my ability at this time.

Farming has essential steps for success. If these steps are not followed, the harvest will be minimal or nothing. Just like farmers must plow the ground for a harvest, people must learn a trade or skill if they wish to earn a decent living. With knowledge expanding at such a rapid rate, people must continually learn to improve their skills.

> "Lazy farmers don't plow when they should; they
> expect a harvest, but there is none."
> Proverbs 20:4

Lack of effort makes it hard to achieve goals. Intelligence without hard work will accomplish little. Hard work and commitment help achieve goals.

> "The lazy will not get what they want,
> but those who work hard will."
> Proverbs 13:4

Jesus worked hard during his three years of public ministry on this earth. Jesus can be an example to people who wish to serve him.

> "Do not be lazy but work hard, serving the
> Lord with all your heart."
> Romans 12:11

The blank lines below provide an opportunity to reflect on how this chapter affected you. Consider using these lines to pause, reflect, and dig deeper on this chapter.

_____

_____

_____

_____

_____

_____

_____

_____

CHAPTER 2

Self-Control

I struggled with self-control for many years of my life. I could be impulsive and speak or take action before thinking it through to consider the possible outcomes.

Part of my maturing and developing as a human being was learning to focus on what I can control, which is myself. Self-control was a challenge when I was insecure about who I was as a person and the principles and values guiding my decisions. I had to learn to stop, take deep breaths, count to ten, and not say or do anything until I had thought and considered possible responses – respond don't react.

When I became comfortable with who I was as a person as well as my strengths and areas for improvement, it was easier to listen and to evaluate input from others with a balanced perspective. My development in this area was a process and a journey that required honesty, open-mindedness, willingness, and discipline. The process and journey was not neat or tidy. Sometimes, the journey was two steps forward and one step backward; other times it was two steps forward and three steps backward. I struggled with perfectionism in my life, which caused me to be my harshest critic at times. I had to learn to be kinder to myself and to judge myself by progress not perfection.

The life lessons that I learned about self-control helped improve relationships with my fellow human beings. The journey was difficult and challenging, but it was worth the time and effort for me. My life is far better with a higher level of self-control. It is a relief not to be so affected by other people's words, actions, and behaviors.

Solomon wrote the book of Proverbs; the book of Proverbs offers suggestions on how to get along with our fellow human beings.

Wisdom and knowledge appear together twice in the verse below. Wisdom and knowledge help a person understand the value of self-control.

2 Chronicles 1:10–12 (New Century Version) reads as follows:

> "Now give me wisdom and knowledge so I can lead these people in the right way, because no one can rule them without your help."

> God said to Solomon, "You have not asked for wealth or riches or honor, or for the death of your enemies, or for a long life. But since you have asked for wisdom and knowledge to lead my people, over whom I have made you king, I will give you wisdom and knowledge. I will also give you more wealth, riches, and honor than any king who has lived before you or any who will live after you."

2 Timothy is the last letter the apostle Paul wrote. When Paul wrote 2 Timothy, Paul was in a Roman prison and he had been sentenced to die. Paul was Timothy's mentor and spiritual father. In 2 Timothy, Paul shared his final thoughts with Timothy, whom Paul loved dearly. Paul wanted 2 Timothy to be practical, inspirational counsel for young Timothy, who had been left to lead the church in Ephesus. Paul exercised self-control in writing 2 Timothy because he did not focus on his circumstances or his impending death. Paul focused on how he could help his beloved Timothy before his death.

"God did not give us a spirit that makes us afraid but
a spirit of power and love and self-control."
2 Timothy 1:7

The blank lines below provide an opportunity to reflect on how this chapter affected you. Consider using these lines to pause, reflect, and dig deeper on this chapter.

_____

_____

_____

_____

_____

_____

_____

_____

_____

_____

_____

_____

_____

_____

_____

_____

_____

_____

_____

_____

_____

CHAPTER 3

Gluttony

There have been times in my life when I have used food to medicate disappointment or unpleasant feelings in my life. Instead of using food to medicate, I need to deal with the disappointment or unpleasant feelings by allowing time to sit with the discomfort, accept that disappointments and unpleasant feelings are part of life, and ask God what he would like me to learn and how God would like me to become a better person.

In the Bible, gluttony means over-indulgence and over-consumption of food, drink, or wealth items, particularly as status symbols. In the past, I have been concerned too much with status symbols like a fancy brief case or a pen. As I have been more comfortable with myself as a person and the principles and values guiding my life, status symbols now have very little meaning or importance. A spiritual awakening has been a significant part of my development in this area.

Eating or drinking excessively can lead to addictions. Addictions can take over a person's life and cause the person to be selfish and self-centered. I drank alcohol for 25 years and I was selfish and self-centered. I quit drinking alcohol 23 years ago, and I am a better person living a better life. Today, I have reached a healthy balance between self-focus and other focus.

"Control yourself if you have a big appetite."
Proverbs 23:2

Moderation is important when drinking alcoholic beverages. If a person becomes addicted to alcoholic beverages, that person has a disease that markedly diminishes the quality of his or her life.

"How terrible it will be for people who are famous for
drinking wine and are champions at mixing drinks."
Isaiah 5:22

Eating and drinking are necessary to sustain life, but there are far more important things in life. God wants to be number one in our lives, and God wants to provide us with rich, abundant lives. Spirituality has been a precious gift that has added richness and meaning to my life; belief in God and prayer are the two driving forces in my life at this time.

"In the kingdom of God, eating and drinking are
not important. The important things are living right
with God, peace, and joy in the Holy Spirit."
Romans 14:17

The blank lines below provide an opportunity to reflect on how this chapter affected you. Consider using these lines to pause, reflect, and dig deeper on this chapter.

CHAPTER 4

Goodness

Goodness is displayed when something is done for another person with no intent of receiving any benefit. My second career as a professional counselor allows me to help people deal with difficult and challenging life issues. When I help a fellow human being, I experience inner emotions that are satisfying and gratifying.

When a person puts their hope in God, God provides the following promise.

> "My hope is in you, so may goodness and honesty guard me."
> Psalm 25:21

When we respect the Lord Jesus, Jesus' goodness is given to us, our children, and our grandchildren. As you read the verse below, think about how respect for Jesus can affect future generations positively.

> "But the Lord's love for those who respect him continues forever
> and ever, and his goodness continues to their grandchildren."
> Psalm 103:17

The verse below shares the progression from faith to goodness to knowledge to self-control to patience to service for God. My spiritual journey has been an amazing and joy-filled process of moving closer to God and to living a life that honors God.

Because you have these blessings, do your best to
add these things to your lives: to your faith, add goodness;
and to your goodness, add knowledge; and to your
knowledge, add self-control; and to your self-control, add
patience; and to your patience, add service for God.
2 Peter 1:5–6

The blank lines below provide an opportunity to reflect on how this chapter affected you. Consider using these lines to pause, reflect, and dig deeper on this chapter.

_____

_____

_____

_____

_____

_____

_____

_____

_____

_____

_____

_____

_____

_____

_____

_____

_____

_____

_____

_____

CHAPTER 5

Greed

Extremes rarely work; seeking the middle ground is generally the best answer. Greed and poverty are the extremes; having enough is the middle ground. There is nothing wrong with having wealth and material possessions as long as God is the first priority in our life.

I have struggled with greed and having too much of my self-worth based on wealth. My wealth has gone up and down – there have times of plenty and lean times. The apostle Paul had helpful commentary on wealth in the verse below.

> "I know how to live when I am poor, and I know how to
> live when I have plenty. I have learned the secret of being
> happy at any time in everything that happens, when I
> have enough to eat and when I go hungry, when I have
> more than I need and when I do not have enough."
> Philippians 4:12 New Century Version (NCV)

Greed is a bottomless pit that is never satisfied. The more money and material possessions a person has, the more the person wants. Greed and material possessions only provide short-term enjoyment. Greed and material possessions will not provide long-term happiness and joy.

> "Greed has two daughters named 'Give' and 'Give.'
> There are three things that are never satisfied, really
> four that never say, 'I've had enough!'"
> Proverbs 30:15

Zacchaeus was a tax collector who became wealthy by being greedy on tax rates he charged. When Zacchaeus met Jesus, Jesus came to his home for dinner. After spending time with Jesus, Zacchaeus was changed, as Luke 19:8–10 (New Century Version) indicates.

> But Zacchaeus stood and said to the Lord, "I will
> give half of my possessions to the poor. And if I have
> cheated anyone, I will pay back four times more."

> Jesus said to him, "Salvation has come to this house today,
> because this man also belongs to the family of Abraham. The
> Son of Man came to find lost people and save them."

As this passage above indicates, greed makes a person feel selfish and empty. All the money Zacchaeus had could not provide the inner peace he desired.

God is interested in the poor, widows, and orphans being helped by their fellow human beings. In the verse below, God encourages generosity to the poor and God asks that greed toward the poor be avoided.

> "If there are poor among you, in one of the towns
> of the land the Lord your God is giving you, do not
> be selfish or greedy toward them. But give freely to
> them, and freely lend them whatever they need."
> Deuteronomy 15:7–8

The blank lines below provide an opportunity to reflect on how this chapter affected you. Consider using these lines to pause, reflect, and dig deeper on this chapter.

_____

_____

_____

_____

CHAPTER 6

Patience

We human beings are not born with patience. The smartphone and computer technology is very helpful and useful, but this technology can encourage immediate gratification. Patience is typically learned by life circumstances.

I learned patience by being married and parenting our daughter. When my wife and I got married, we had to deal with differences, negotiate, compromise, and get used to each other's idiosyncrasies. It was one thing to date, it was another thing to live in the same home. It took patience and a willingness to change and adapt. I thought marriage was a major life adjustment until our daughter was born. A child changes everything in life and it took patience on both my wife and my part as we learned how to be parents and how our couples relationship changed based on being parents.

Patience is valuable in dealing with our fellow human beings and in dealing with challenging situations. Patience properly displayed can diffuse volatile situations. As I have learned to "keep calm and carry on," my ability to deal with difficult people and stressful situations has improved.

> "With patience you can convince a ruler, and a gentle
> word can get through to the hard-headed."
> Proverbs 25:15

The apostle Paul wrote the verse below and shared a truth that can be difficult to learn. The sequence of events in the passage below is fascinating. What begins with troubles ends with hope and is dependent upon learning patience and character while going through the process. I have learned more in difficult and challenging situations than I have learned when times were good and relatively easy.

> "We also have joy with our troubles, because we know
> that these troubles produce patience. And patience
> produces character, and character produces hope."
> Romans 5:3–4

The apostle John was exiled to the island of Patmos because he refused to stop preaching the gospel of Jesus Christ. Many of the other apostles were killed for preaching about Jesus. The apostle Paul endured suffering for preaching the gospel of Jesus. All the apostles displayed patience in continuing to preach the gospel of Jesus despite the suffering and the hardships.

> "I, John, am your brother. All of us share with Christ in
> suffering, in the kingdom, and in patience to continue.
> I was on the island of Patmos, because I had preached
> the word of God and the message about Jesus."
> Revelation 1:9

The blank lines below provide an opportunity to reflect on how this chapter affected you. Consider using these lines to pause, reflect, and dig deeper on this chapter

_____

_____

_____

_____

_____

_____

CHAPTER 7

Envy

Envy is a feeling of discontent or resentful longing aroused by someone else's possessions, qualities, or luck. If we compare ourselves to others, we will generally fall short in one or more areas. Instead of comparing ourselves to others, have an attitude of gratitude for what God has provided us. I confess being guilty in this area too many times. Instead of envy, I should have been focused on the gifts God gave me and how God wished me to use those gifts. When I was being envious, I never experienced inner peace or joy.

I was surprised that envy only generated six verses from the Bible. When a person envies another human being, that person assumes that he or she knows the other human being thoroughly, but that is generally not true. One person rarely knows what the other person is thinking, what the other person feels inside, and what happens behind closed doors at the person's home. Outward appearances can be deceiving.

It can be difficult not to envy sinners when they appear to be prospering and enjoying life. Looks can be deceiving - people can put on good appearances and conceal their problems.

> "Don't envy sinners, but always respect the Lord.
> Then you will have hope for the future,
> and your wishes will come true."
> Proverbs 23:17–18

The people with whom we associate can influence our thoughts, feelings, emotions, and behavior. We need to carefully consider the people whom we call friends. Principles and values are two factors to consider in selecting friends.

While Jesus was on this earth, he associated with sinners and evil people. We should follow Jesus' example of wanting to help sinners and evil people, but we need to be cautious about letting sinners and evil people from negatively affecting us.

> "Don't envy evil people or try to be friends with them.
> Their minds are always planning violence, and
> they always talk about making trouble."
> Proverbs 24:1–2

Sometimes we may wonder why God allows evil and wicked people to prosper and to not experience negative consequences for their behavior. This verse lets us know that God is aware of the actions of evil and wicked people and that, one day, God will deal with them on their transgressions.

> "Don't envy evil people, and don't be jealous of the wicked.
> An evil person has nothing to hope for; the wicked
> will die like a flame that is put out."
> Proverbs 24:19–20

The blank lines below provide an opportunity to reflect on how this chapter affected you. Consider using these lines to pause, reflect, and dig deeper on this chapter.

_____

_____

_____

_____

_____

CHAPTER 8

Joy

Happiness is based on life circumstances, so happiness can come and go quickly. Happiness can be affected by people, places, and things. Joy is based on understanding that God created us, and God loves us beyond our human understanding. People can have joy during trials, tribulations, and suffering if they remember that God will be with us during these situations, that these situations will pass, and that God will develop and improve our character through these situations. For too many years, my life was based on happiness rather than joy. It took me some time to learn that trials, tribulation, and suffering could be valuable learning experiences in helping me mature personally and spiritually if I had the proper attitude.

God hates sin, but God loves the sinner. The passage below indicates how much God values people who confess their sins to God and ask God to forgive their sins. God is pleased when people change their lives after being forgiven of their sins. I have learned that it is better for me to confess sooner rather than later. I have embraced that honesty is the best policy and that honesty provides peace and joy.

> "In the same way, I tell you there is more joy in heaven
> over one sinner who changes his heart and life, than over
> ninety-nine good people who do not need to change."
> Luke 15:7

For any meaningful relationship in our life – spouse, children, parents, grandparents, there will be times when we will be challenged by negative feelings and emotions. It can be difficult to forgive another person who has hurt us, but it is important to forgive. There have several instances in my life when I have asked God to help me forgive another person because my stubborn human flesh did not want to forgive. In each instance, God has helped me forgive and I have experienced relief and inner peace along with the relationship being improved. When I have granted forgiveness, the prisoner was released, and the prisoner was me.

The passage below provides joy during the midst of trials and tribulations because God is walking with us. During difficult times in my life, my faith and my relationship with God have improved when I have asked God to help me. I have felt comfort and peace knowing that God is with me in the difficult issue.

> "Even if I walk through a very dark valley, I will
> not be afraid, because you are with me. Your rod
> and your shepherd's staff comfort me."
> Psalm 23:4

In spite of the difficulties encountered in his ministry, Paul continued to share the good news of Jesus Christ with the world. Paul understood his life priorities and he was committed to pursue his life priorities regardless of the cost. Paul was able to remain joyful during his trials, tribulations, and suffering because of his relationship with God and the joy provided by the Holy Spirit.

> "Five times the Jews have given me their punishment
> of thirty-nine lashes with a whip. Three different times
> I was beaten with rods. One time I was almost stoned to
> death. Three times I was in ships that wrecked, and one
> of those times I spent a night and a day in the sea."
> 2 Corinthians 11:24-25 (New Century Version)

The blank lines below provide an opportunity to reflect on how this chapter affected you. Consider using these lines to pause, reflect, and dig deeper on this chapter.

CHAPTER 9

Lust

Lust is a very strong sexual desire for someone. Lust tends to focus on physical attraction only. Earlier in my life, I have looked at females with lust. After being married and having a daughter, I have come to realize that there is more to sex in a relationship than only the physical aspect of sex. Sexual fulfillment is most satisfying when intimacy exists emotionally, spiritually, and physically.

God created men and women to be attracted to each other. God created Adam in the garden of Eden. When God saw that Adam was lonely, God created Eve. God supports love, romance, and marriage. The Song of Solomon in the Bible is a love story between a man and a woman. Song of Solomon 7:1–9 (New Century Version) reads as follows:

"The Man Speaks to the Woman

Your feet are beautiful in sandals, you daughter of a prince.
Your round thighs are like jewels shaped by an artist.
Your navel is like a round drinking cup always filled with wine.
Your stomach is like a pile of wheat surrounded with lilies.
Your breasts are like two fawns, like twins of a gazelle.
Your neck is like an ivory tower.
Your eyes are like the pools in Heshbon near the gate of Bath Rabbim.
Your nose is like the mountain of Lebanon that looks down on Damascus.

Your head is like Mount Carmel, and your hair is like purple cloth; the king is captured in its folds.
You are beautiful and pleasant; my love, you are full of delights.
You are tall like a palm tree, and your breasts are like its bunches of fruit.
I said, "I will climb up the palm tree and take hold of its fruit." Let your breasts be like bunches of grapes, the smell of your breath like apples, and your mouth like the best wine.

The Woman Speaks to the Man

Let this wine go down sweetly for my lover; may it flow gently past the lips and teeth."

The verses above express love between the husband and the wife in intimate details. God supports sexual intimacy within marriage.

Sexual attraction is a powerful force between two people. Lust is possible for any human being. Lust can lead to pornography, adultery, and prostitution. Some possible negative consequences of lust are extramarital affairs, divorce, pregnancy outside marriage, and sexually transmitted diseases.

The blank lines below provide an opportunity to reflect on how this chapter affected you. Consider using these lines to pause, reflect, and dig deeper on this chapter.

_____

_____

_____

_____

_____

_____

_____

_____

CHAPTER 10

Kindness

The Golden Rule is "Treat other people the way you wish to be treated." The Golden Rule is one example of kindness. I have embraced the Golden Rule in my life, it has improved the quality of my relationships, and it has provided joy and peace.

Kindness is a choice each person makes. In God's economy, we will reap what we sow, we will reap more than we sow, and we will reap longer than we sow. If a person sows kindness, kindness will return to that person. If a person sows evil and wickedness, evil and wickedness will return to that person. In my life, I have sowed anger and kindness. When I have used a harsh start-up with critical comments, the other person has generally responded defensively and nothing productive has been accomplished. When I choose to begin with kindness and use a soft start-up characterized by words that encourage an end result that will benefit everyone, the other person is more willing to listen and to work collaboratively on a solution.

> "Whoever looks for good will find kindness, but
> whoever looks for evil will find trouble."
> Proverbs 11:27

Compassion and empathy are forms of kindness. When I am working with clients as a counselor, compassion and empathy can give the person being helped a boost when he or she really needs it. The person who receives compassion and empathy is blessed as well as the person who gives compassion and empathy.

The Bible discusses two women who were widows – Naomi, the mother-in-law and her daughter-in-law Ruth. Naomi had three significant deaths in her life – her husband and her two sons. After Ruth's husband died, Ruth traveled to a foreign land with Naomi and Ruth cared for Naomi. Boaz was a wealthy relative of Naomi, and he was a bachelor. Naomi sent Ruth to sleep at the foot of Boaz and use Boaz's blanket to cover her. Boaz was grateful for Ruth's act of sleeping at his feet and covering herself with Boaz's blanket. Boaz asked Ruth to marry him, so Naomi had two people to watch over and care for her. Boaz and Ruth had a son after marriage, so Naomi became a grandmother.

Ruth's kindness came back to her from both Naomi and Boaz. Ruth was selfless in helping Naomi and in moving to a foreign country with Naomi. Kindness is a boomerang that comes back to the person initially showing kindness.

> Then Boaz said, "The LORD bless you, my daughter.
> This act of kindness is greater than the kindness you
> showed to Naomi in the beginning. You didn't look for a
> young man to marry, either rich or poor. Now, my daughter,
> don't be afraid. I will do everything you ask, because all
> the people in our town know you are a good woman."
> Ruth 3:10–11

Jonathan was the son of Saul, the king who was jealous of David and who tried to kill David for many years. Jonathan and David were friends despite Saul's evil intentions for David. After David became king, David allowed Jonathan's son, Mephibosheth, to always eat at David's table, and David gave back all the land of his grandfather Saul. David valued his friendship with Jonathan more than any ill feelings toward Saul. David showed kindness to Mephibosheth the remaining days of his life. David's kindness to Mephibosheth was important because Mephibosheth was crippled in both feet.

> "The king asked, 'Is anyone left in Saul's family? I want to show God's kindness to that person.' Ziba answered the king, 'Jonathan has a son still living who is crippled in both feet.'"
>
> 2 Samuel 9:3

It takes a person who is both personally mature and spiritually mature to look past wrongs done by another human being and to show kindness toward that person or a member of that person's family.

During Jesus' public ministry on this earth, Jesus ate and associated with sinners. Jesus' ministry made it clear that Jesus came to save not only people living good lives but also sinners.

Some people are intimidated by churches because they think churches contain only perfect people who are living good lives. There are no perfect people; we have all sinned and fallen short. The only person who lived on this earth and did not sin was our Lord and Savior, Jesus Christ. Churches form a group of imperfect people living with other imperfect people in an imperfect world. If churches viewed themselves as God's spiritual hospital, they would welcome sinners.

The blank lines below provide an opportunity to reflect on how this chapter affected you. Consider using these lines to pause, reflect, and dig deeper on this chapter.

_____

_____

_____

_____

_____

_____

_____

CHAPTER 11

Faithfulness

Faithfulness with family, friends, and colleagues is valued, particularly in difficult and stressful circumstances. It is nice to know someone "has our back." I have personally experienced this level of support. I am so grateful to have had people in my life that loved and cared for me enough to be there regardless of the issues.

When an important person in our life has hurt us, we may need to tell them: "I love you, but I do not like your attitude, words, or behavior at this time." I have had to adopt this stance several times during my life. These words were not easy for me to say. I have tried to Speak the TRUTH in Love to let the person know that I value them as a person, but I have concerns about their words, actions, or behaviors. Speak the TRUTH in Love can share comments with compassion and empathy while still communicating the message assertively. Below are some comments about TRUTH.

- T – Think it over. Carefully consider the words to say.
- R – Reveal your heart – show compassion and empathy.
- U – Understand the other person's position. If you were the person receiving the message rather than the person delivering the message, what words would you like to be said and how would you like it to be said – tone of voice, place, time.
- T – Tell it like it is. Don't beat around the bush so much that the person receiving the message does not understand what is being communicated.

- H – Hold up hope. Communicate that you believe person is capable of making change requested.

In the book of Exodus, Moses led the Israelites after they were freed from Egyptian slavery. In Exodus 34 (New Century Version), God gave Moses new stone tablets with the Ten Commandments. God displayed faithfulness to the Israelites by providing a second set of stone tablets with the Ten Commandments. The Ten Commandments provided guidance and direction to the Israelites on how to relate to their fellow human beings and on how to relate to God. God was faithful in communicating his directions for living a life that was meaningful and beneficial.

"The Lord passed in front of Moses and said, 'I am the Lord. The Lord is a God who shows mercy, who is kind, who doesn't become angry quickly, who has great love and faithfulness.'"
Exodus 34:6

God displays his faithfulness to humanity by being loving, kind, merciful, and slow to anger as indicated by the verse below.

"But, Lord, you are a God who shows mercy and is kind. You don't become angry quickly. You have great love and faithfulness."
Psalm 86:15

Faithfulness is an important attribute in any long-term relationship with another human being or with God. Family members, relatives, friends, and colleagues are important human relationships. Loyalty and commitment are two aspects of faithfulness. Faithfulness is particularly valued when other human beings and God support and help us during challenging times of our life.

The blank lines below provide an opportunity to reflect on how this chapter affected you. Consider using these lines to pause, reflect, and dig deeper on this chapter.

CHAPTER 12

Anger

When I am angry, I am not thinking clearly. I had to learn the importance of calming down before saying or doing anything. I had to learn to count to ten and take deep breaths. I had to think about the desired end result of communication and ask myself if the next words out of my mouth were moving me farther away or closer to my desired end result.

For many years, I had a passive aggressive style of communication. When I was passive, I let my frustrations and disappointments accumulate until I could hold no more, and then the volcano erupted. My volcanos damaged or ended several relationships. Anger did nothing to improve my relationships with other human beings. I had to learn assertive communication, which is the middle ground between passive and aggressive. Assertive communication addresses issues timely and Speak the TRUTH in Love is one tool.

When I am angry and the communication is not going well, time out is one possible option to let all parties calm down before discussing the matter further. For a time out, all parties need to go to separate locations for an agreed upon time like 15 or 30 minutes with the goal of calming down. Time outs can help disagreements from escalating to very damaging communication.

Anger and jealousy can be a dangerous combination, as indicated by the passage below.

"Anger kills the fool, and jealousy slays the stupid."
Job 5:2

The apostle Paul was a great evangelist as well as the writer of many books in the New Testament. In the verse below, the apostle Paul encourages us to put anger, bad temper, and hurtful words or actions against another person out of our life, so we can have the rich, abundant life God wants us to live.

"But now also put these things out of your life:
anger, bad temper, doing or saying things to hurt
others, and using evil words when you talk."
Colossians 3:8

The only person I can control is myself. When another person becomes angry with me, I have the choice to remain calm or the choice to join the other person in anger. I have found that taking a deep breath, counting to ten, and thinking, *Respond, don't react,* before saying or doing anything has helped me deal with anger much better. When I am able to remain calm with an angry person, I am able to create an environment where the other person may be able to regain her or his composure.

"A gentle answer will calm a person's anger, but
an unkind answer will cause more anger."
Proverbs 15:1

The blank lines below provide an opportunity to reflect on how this chapter affected you. Consider using these lines to pause, reflect, and dig deeper on this chapter.

_____

_____

_____

_____

CHAPTER 13

Gentleness

In any situation, what would you like the end result to be? Are the next words out of your mouth moving you closer to or farther away from your desired end result?

When I choose gentleness when dealing with people and situations, my gentleness makes people more receptive to listening and to cooperating. When I begin with critical comments and/or anger, I have little likelihood of calming down the situation, or coming to a collaborative solution with the people affected. When I choose gentleness, the end result has always been better for the other people involved and me. Gentleness for me begins with a calm and soft tone of voice followed by positive and supportive words.

In the verse below, gentleness is surrounded by mercy, kindness, humility, and patience – what an awesome combination of attributes.

> "God has chosen you and made you his holy people. He
> loves you. So you should always clothe yourselves with
> mercy, kindness, humility, gentleness, and patience."
> Colossians 3:12

The apostle Paul was Timothy's spiritual father and mentor. In the following verse, Paul is sharing insightful comments with his beloved Timothy, a fellow minister of the gospel. Paul's love and concern for Timothy come through in the wisdom shared.

"But you, man of God, run away from all those things.
Instead, live in the right way, serve God, have
faith, love, patience, and gentleness."
1 Timothy 6:11

Gentleness, wisdom, and understanding are signs of personal maturity and spiritual maturity. The verse below shares some insights worth considering.

"Are there those among you who are truly wise and
understanding? Then they should show it by living right and
doing good things with a gentleness that comes from wisdom."
James 3:13

The blank lines below provide an opportunity to reflect on how this chapter affected you. Consider using these lines to pause, reflect, and dig deeper on this chapter.

_____

_____

_____

_____

_____

_____

_____

_____

_____

_____

_____

_____

_____

_____

_____

CHAPTER 14

Our world today has so much negativity and divisiveness that experiencing peace can be a challenge. Life is a balancing act for me – being aware of what is going on in our world without getting so upset and feeling stressed all the time. Some tools that help keep me at peace are exercise, spending time outdoors, limiting the information and time spent on world events, spending quiet time with God, and praying to God for guidance and direction in my life.

I find that peace leads to contentment with my life and encourages me to live in harmony with my fellow human beings. Peace helps me remain calm during trying and difficult situations. I see peace as a gift from God for living a life that honors God.

> "Obey God and be at peace with him;
> this is the way to happiness."
> Job 22:21

"Actions speak louder than words" is a powerful statement. People listen to the words from our mouths; people view our actions and determine if our actions are consistent with our words and if they wish to live as we do. Inner peace can sustain me regardless of my worldly circumstances. When people see me being at peace in difficult and stressful situations, they may ask me how I can have inner peace, and it creates an opportunity for me to share my spirituality.

"When people live so that they please the Lord, even
their enemies will make peace with them."
Proverbs 16:7

Jesus shared the verse below with his followers, so they could experience peace despite enduring difficult life circumstances. Jesus understood that this world could be difficult and troubling at times.

"I leave you peace; my peace I give you. I do not give it to you as
the world does. So don't let your hearts be troubled or afraid."
John 14:27

The verse below encourages us to live in peace with other people as best we can. Not everyone is going to like us. Some people may be difficult or hostile in their dealings with us. The verse below does not expect perfection in our relationships with other people because perfection is not possible in our fallen world. The verse below does request that we give our best effort to live in peace.

"Do your best to live in peace with everyone."
Romans 12:18

The only person I can control is me. When people say or do things that irritate me, I have the choice how to respond. Proverbs 15:1 (New Century Version) states, "A gentle answer will calm a person's anger, but an unkind answer will cause more anger."

The blank lines below provide an opportunity to reflect on how this chapter affected you. Consider using these lines to pause, reflect, and dig deeper on this chapter.

_____

_____

_____

_____

CHAPTER 15

Pride

A number of years ago, our church was building a larger church and church members were permitted to write their favorite Bible verse on the concrete floor before the carpet was laid. At that time, I did not have a favorite Bible verse, so I asked Jesus to provide the Bible verse he wanted for me. When Jesus provided Proverbs 16:18, it was a wake-up call for me.

"Pride leads to destruction; a proud attitude brings ruin."
Proverbs 16:18

After reading Proverbs 16:18, I asked Jesus to help me learn where Jesus wanted me to improve and Jesus did. I learned to have a better balance between being self-focused and other-focused – think about what is best for everyone affected by the issue and do the next right thing.

Another help for me in dealing with my pride was Billy Graham's prayer (*Day by Day with Billy Graham*) for Proverbs 16:18, which follows: "Lord, deliver me from the sin of pride and fill me with continuing humility as I go about the tasks before me this day." If I feel pride trying to puff me up, I stop and pray Billy Graham's prayer, then pride departs and inner peace returns.

It is easy to display pride; it is hard to practice humility. Humility requires self-control; humility provides the gift of inner peace.

"When you do things, do not let selfishness
or pride be your guide. Instead, be humble and give
more honor to others than to yourselves."
Philippians 2:3

Pride is one of the seven deadly sins and many people consider it the most dangerous of the seven deadly sins. Pride can lead a person to the other six deadly sins, which are envy, anger, greed, gluttony, lust, and laziness.

"Keep me from the sins of pride; don't let them rule me.
Then I can be pure and innocent of the greatest of sins."
Psalm 19:13

The apostle Paul was Timothy's spiritual father and mentor. In the following verse, the apostle Paul is communicating with Timothy, a fellow pastor, about the dangers of pride.

"This person is full of pride and understands nothing but is sick
with a love for arguing and fighting about words. This brings
jealousy, fighting, speaking against others, evil mistrust."
1 Timothy 6:4

Pride can make a person feel more important than he or she is. Pride caused the devil Satan to rebel against God. Pride can cause a person to believe that he or she has no need for God. Pride leads to destruction and ruin. Pride may be the most dangerous of the seven deadly sins.

For many years, I struggled with pride. When I sought to improve my spirituality through spending quiet time with God, studying the Bible, praying, and attending church worship service, God helped me identify pride in my life and taught me how to reduce pride in my life. With pride, I need to take some of the focus off of me and my interests and have a better balance of self-focus and focus on others and what is best for everyone involved. By allowing the Holy Spirit to teach me the Fruit of the Spirit and how to apply the Fruit of the Spirit in my life, I have become a better person living a better life.

Pride and inner peace cannot co-exist. I value inner peace more than pride.

The blank lines below provide an opportunity to reflect on how this chapter affected you. Consider using these lines to pause, reflect, and dig deeper on this chapter.

_____

_____

_____

_____

_____

_____

_____

_____

_____

_____

_____

_____

_____

_____

_____

_____

_____

_____

_____

_____

_____

_____

_____

CHAPTER 16

People and relationships add richness, meaning, and purpose to life. Love hopefully exists in important human relationships – parents, spouse, children, grandparents, siblings, and friends.

1 Corinthians 13:4-7 (New Century Version) describes love.

> "Love is patient and kind. Love is not jealous, it does not brag, and it is not proud. [5] Love is not rude, is not selfish, and does not get upset with others. Love does not count up wrongs that have been done. [6] Love takes no pleasure in evil but rejoices over the truth. [7] Love patiently accepts all things. It always trusts, always hopes, and always endures."

Agape love is the highest form of love. Agape love is the love of God for man and hopefully man for God.

The verse below captures the very essence of God. God is love; human beings are capable of loving only because God made us in his image. If a person does not love others, the apostle John says that that person does not know God.

"Whoever does not love does not know God, because God is love."
1 John 4:8 (New Century Version)

God displayed his love for humanity when he allowed his only Son, Jesus Christ, to enter our sinful world and ultimately die a painful death on the cross. As a parent, I cannot imagine seeing my only child suffer an excruciating death like execution on the cross. Jesus' passion and death paid the sin debt in full for all people. Salvation is a precious gift from Jesus: we do not deserve it, and we cannot earn it. If a person accepts Jesus as their Lord and Savior, that person will spend eternity in heaven with Jesus.

"God loved the world so much that he gave his one
and only Son so that whoever believes in him
may not be lost but have eternal life."
John 3:16

Jesus possessed an amazing gift to be able to summarize important concepts in few words. In the passage below, Jesus condensed all the Jewish laws of his time into two concepts: love God and love your neighbor as yourself.

Jesus said, "What is written in the law?
What do you read there?"

The man answered, "Love the Lord your God with all
your heart, all your soul, all your strength, and all your
mind." Also, "Love your neighbor as you love yourself."

Jesus said to him, "Your answer is right.
Do this and you will live."
Luke 10:26–28

Every one of us has said something or done something that we wish had not happened. We have all experienced guilt and shame over words spoken or behaviors exhibited. The verse below reminds us that God loves us regardless of what we have said or done. God not only loves us, but God is willing to forgive our transgressions if we confess our failures to him with humility and if we ask to be forgiven.

> "Nothing above us, nothing below us, nor anything else
> in the whole world will ever be able to separate us from
> the love of God that is in Christ Jesus our Lord."
> Romans 8:39

The book of Philemon is the shortest book in the Bible, but it displays our human condition in amazing detail. The book of Philemon is a letter from the apostle Paul to Philemon. Philemon owned a slave named Onesimus, who ran away and became friends with Paul. In biblical times, a slave who ran away from his master could be severely punished. Paul made Onesimus return to Philemon with a letter from Paul asking Philemon to show mercy on Onesimus because of the help Paul provided Philemon in Philemon's spiritual journey. Onesimus represents those of us who sinned and who could do nothing to save ourselves. Philemon represents God the Father, who hates sin. Paul represents our Lord and Savior, Jesus Christ, who paid our sin debt in full by his death at Calvary. The cross at Calvary was where the wrath of God the Father for humanity's sins met the righteousness of God as expressed in Jesus Christ. When a person accepts Jesus as their Lord and Savior, their sins are forgiven and when God the Father views this person, God the Father sees the person as pure due to the shed blood of Jesus washing away the person's sins.

> "But because I love you, I am pleading with you instead. I,
> Paul, an old man now and also a prisoner for Christ Jesus."
> Philemon 1:9

Love provides richness and meaning to life. I admit that love can sometimes be a challenge because I am an imperfect human being living with other imperfect beings in an imperfect world. I do not always say or do everything right. When other people can be challenging and difficult to deal with, I can struggle wanting to love them. However, the alternatives of hate and unforgiveness are poison to me and they rob me of things I value more – inner peace and joy.

The blank lines below provide an opportunity to reflect on how this chapter affected you. Consider using these lines to pause, reflect, and dig deeper on this chapter.

_____

_____

_____

_____

_____

_____

_____

_____

_____

_____

_____

_____

_____

_____

_____

_____

_____

_____

_____

_____

_____

_____

_____

_____

_____

CHAPTER 17

Final Thoughts

Thank you for reading this book and taking this journey about the principles and values that will guide your life and your life decisions. I hope the journey has been meaningful and beneficial.

If you have chosen to write comments on the pages for reflection and digging deeper, I hope you will go back, read what you have written, and think about the life you find worth living going forward.

Negativity and divisiveness permeate our world today. Think how much different our world today and our relationships with our fellow human beings could be if people avoided the Seven Deadly Sins and if people embraced the Fruit of the Spirit.

The choices we make determine the life paths we travel. When I have made poor choices and unwise decisions, I have said and done things that caused regret and guilt. When I have made better choices and wiser decisions, the outcomes have been far more satisfying – better relationships with my fellow human beings, inner peace, liked the person I saw in the mirror. I have done some things my way and I have done some things God's way – the end results have been far better when I have done things God's way.

At this time in my life, God and prayer are my top two life priorities. Key principles guiding my life are the Golden Rule, the Ten Commandments, and Stephen Covey's Seven Habits of Highly Effective People.

If people followed the Golden Rule and the Ten Commandments, think about how different our world might be today.

I was raised in a strict religious background. There were rules and there were negative consequences for violating the rules. My early religion was about checking the proper boxes and avoiding punishment. I did not see God as a loving person, and I did not have a personal relationship with God.

At this time in my life, I have my morning coffee with God. I read my daily devotional, I talk with God, I listen to God, I pray for others and myself, I ask God for guidance and direction for that day, I ask God how I can serve him this day, and I ask God to help me be the person he wants me to be this day. I have a personal relationship with God and that personal relationship has dramatically changed my life and my outlook on life.

I am still an imperfect human being living with other imperfect human beings in an imperfect world. I still have life situations and people that are challenging.

I am a work in progress, and I will continue to be a work in progress as long as I am on this earth. With God's help, I am trying to become a better person each day.

The most important decision I made in my life was to accept Jesus Christ as my Lord and Savior. Because of that decision, I do not fear death and I know that I will spend eternity in heaven with God. That decision gives me inner peace that surpasses all human understanding.

Spirituality is based on a personal relationship with a loving God. I would encourage you to explore that area of your life and decide if you wish to make any changes. God created us human beings with a free will. God will not force himself upon you, but God stands ready, willing, and able to welcome you and to love you like no one has ever loved you.

This book presents two possible life paths – the Seven Deadly Sins and the Fruit of the Spirit. The choices we make with our free will determine the life paths we will travel and the people and life experiences we will have. I hope you make choices that provide you with a life you value and a life that provides meaning and purpose.

REFERENCES

Brown, Joan Winmill. *Day by Day with Billy Graham.* World Wide Publications. Minneapolis, Minnesota, 1976.

Lucado, Max, ed. *The Devotional Bible: Experiencing the Heart of Jesus.* New Century Version. Nashville, Tennessee: Thomas Nelson, Inc., 2003.

ABOUT THE AUTHOR

Edward Craven lives in the Atlanta, Georgia metropolitan area.

Edward Craven is an empty nester and a widower with one daughter.

Edward Craven finished the final manuscript for this book shortly before leaving for a bucket list trip to Israel with about 50 people from his church.

Edward Craven is a Licensed Professional Counselor in Georgia.

CPSIA information can be obtained
at www.ICGtesting.com
Printed in the USA
BVHW031627240820
587139BV00003B/500

9 781951 469337